THE LBSCR ELEVATED ELECTRIFICATION

a pictorial view of construction

Noodle Books

PUBLISHERS NOTE

The origins of this book, so far as the present publisher is concerned, may be traced back perhaps five or so years, to the time I was starting on what is the associated 'Southern Way' series.

At that point I was on the look out for potential material and came across a reference on a railways auction site to two albums of LBSCR material from the estate of the late R C Riley. I was successful in my bid and on collecting the items was advised a further two volumes would be likely to appear in a subsequent sale. Again I was successful and so became the proud owner of a series of well worn, large format volumes, which included most of the material seen within these pages.

The intention of course was to provide an archive of material for the aforementioned 'Southern Way' series, although to date just two brief illustrative pieces have appeared, in issues 4 and 6 - neither related to electrification.

It quickly became apparent there was a problem with what to do with the bulk of the illustrations depicting the construction of the 'Brighton Overhead'. There were no accompanying notes, save for a few words on most of the images reference the actual location, whilst my own knowledge of the subject was limited.

Here Stephen Grant came to the rescue, a chance conversation on a totally unrelated subject and Stephen kindly came back with the offer to caption the material. As an enthusiast for the subject, he is the ideal man to undertake the task and I am extremely grateful to him. How long the albums might otherwise have lain gathering their share of dust can only be imagined.

Having discussed the subjects shown with Stephen we have come to a mutual conclusion. The actual volumes were clearly once part of an official archive, possibly even in the records of the LBSCR electrical or civil engineer, they have also passed through several hands, as the binding is either non existent or in poor repair, although we must be grateful for the fact they have survived at all.

Clearly they only show part of the work that went on, rolling stock for example is conspicuous by its absence, although the obvious bonus is that as far as we are aware the majority of the images should be new to the reader.

It is the intention is that eventually the four albums will be deposited with the Bluebell Archive.

Kevin Robertson

The Brighton Elevated Electrification

Introduction

This is the story, told through official photographs taken at the time, of one of the earliest railway electrification projects in the world. As we shall see, it was not the first and its a.c. overhead infrastructure was to be short lived, replaced by the Southern Railway's standard d.c. third rail system within 20 years. Nevertheless, these pictures provide a fascinating insight into the application of Edwardian electrical engineering technology to a busy London suburban railway.

The South London Suburban Network

The 19th century steam suburban railway had given millions the opportunity to commute to work in London whilst living and raising a family away from the smoke, pollution and disease of the inner city.

The London, Brighton and South Coast Railway (LBSCR), formed in 1846, actively developed the market for suburban travel. Wealthy London merchants had already built large villas in the hills to the south of London, served from 1839 by one of the LBSCR's progenitors, the London & Croydon Railway. The area was given a considerable boost when Paxton's Crystal Palace, originally built in Hyde Park for the Great Exhibition of 1851, was reconstructed in 1854 near Sydenham as a venue for concerts and exhibitions. The Crystal Palace, set amid gardens and parklands with statues and spectacular fountains, soon became a popular destination for Victorian days out.

In that same year the LBSCR opened a short branch linking its main line from London Bridge to a handsome new Crystal Palace station to serve this lucrative traffic. Two years later the line was extended from Crystal Palace through a 750-yard tunnel under Sydenham Hill and onwards to a point near the present Clapham Junction. In 1860 this line was further extended across the Thames to a new, six-platform Victoria station in London's West End. The Victoria and London Bridge lines formed the framework for a dense network, mostly built during the 1850s and 1860s, that fed and was fed by a boom in house construction on what had previously been open country.

Electric Traction

It was at Crystal Palace in 1881 that Werner von Siemens demonstrated the electric locomotive he had first shown at the 1879 Berlin Industrial Exhibition and a 20-inch gauge electric line seems to have operated in the grounds of Crystal Palace intermittently until 1884. Meanwhile Magnus Volk, Victorian inventor and Brighton resident, was also investigating the possibilities of electricity for rail traction and in 1883 he opened a demonstration electric railway along the Brighton seafront. The Volks Electric Railway, much rebuilt, is still operating today.

Electric traction came of age in England with the opening in 1890 of the City & South London Railway, London's first deep-level tube. In 1892 Leeds became the first city to operate electric trams and a year later the all-electric Liverpool Overhead Railway started operations.

The new technology offered very significant potential benefits to railway operators. Electric suburban trains could accelerate faster than their steam-hauled counterparts, not only offering shorter journey times but also allowing more trains to operate over busy stretches of line.

Front cover - *Linesmen and labourers prepare for the day's work in the Down yard at Tulse Hill. A train is signalled on the Down Portsmouth line through the junction ahead.*
Front cover inset - *A completed train for the South London Line. See also page 25.*
Title page - *Cantilever masts are in place over the two South London Line tracks at Cambria Junction in November 1907. Looking eastwards towards Denmark Hill, the two tracks on the left are used by London Chatham and Dover Railway (LCDR) services over the Catford Loop. The converging lines form the Cambria Spur from Loughborough Junction on the LCDR route from Holborn Viaduct to Herne Hill. This part of the South London Line was built as a joint venture. The LBSCR was responsible for all four tracks from Cow Lane, east of Peckham Rye, to Barrington Road Junction, just behind the photographer, and the LCDR provided the four tracks from that point onwards to Factory Junction, where the South London Line diverged from the LCDR route to Victoria via Stewarts Lane and continued on a brick viaduct to join the Brighton main line at Battersea Park. The practice of cutting a distinguishing 'fishtail' notch into the arms of distant signals was first adopted by the LBSCR in 1872 and soon became a Board of Trade requirement for all companies. However it was not until the 1920s that yellow arms and lights were generally adopted by British main line railways to distinguish these advance warning signals from stop signals.*

Terminal capacity was another constraint on the steam suburban railway. A train arrives, another engine backs down and couples up, the train departs and the original engine follows it out - four movements instead of the two needed for an electric multiple unit. Even with the slickest operation, platform re-occupation times were several minutes longer for locomotive-hauled trains than for electric multiple units whilst the associated light engine movements and refuge sidings consumed track capacity in the station throat.

Multiple unit trains could be joined together to form longer trains at peak times whilst maintaining broadly constant power-to-weight ratios and, with more driven axles and a steady torque applied to those axles, it was easier to maintain adhesion on steep gradients or slippery rails.

With no need for separate locomotives and with most of the electrical equipment under the floor, almost all of the train length, and therefore the terminal platform length, was available for a payload of passengers or luggage.

Electric traction also needed less time in the depot for servicing and maintenance so the fleet could be utilised more intensively and, of course, there was a considerable cost saving in eliminating the need for a fireman on each train.

The LBSCR Electrification System

With all of these advantages, electrification was attracting the attention of railway company directors throughout the world but the LBSCR Board was, perhaps, spurred into immediate action by a 1900 proposal to build a new, non-stop electric railway from London to Brighton with a promised journey time of 50 minutes. This particular scheme came to nothing but within two years the LBSCR had obtained Parliamentary powers to electrify its entire network.

The company therefore needed an system that was suitable for electrifying its main lines through to Brighton, Eastbourne and Portsmouth as well as facilitating faster and more frequent suburban services. This was undoubtedly a factor in the advice of Sir Philip Dawson, the LBSCR's Consulting Electrical Engineer, to adopt a single-phase a.c. system with a relatively high nominal 6,600 Volt tension and with the option of stepping up to 11,000 Volts at a later date. A high-tension system would enable feeder stations to be more widely spaced, helping to equalise the load in open country where trains would be less frequent. As there were insufficient clearances for such high voltages at track level, as staff on the line would need protection from flashovers and as the voltage drop over distance would be much greater for conductor rails than for copper wire, power was supplied to trains by overhead catenary.

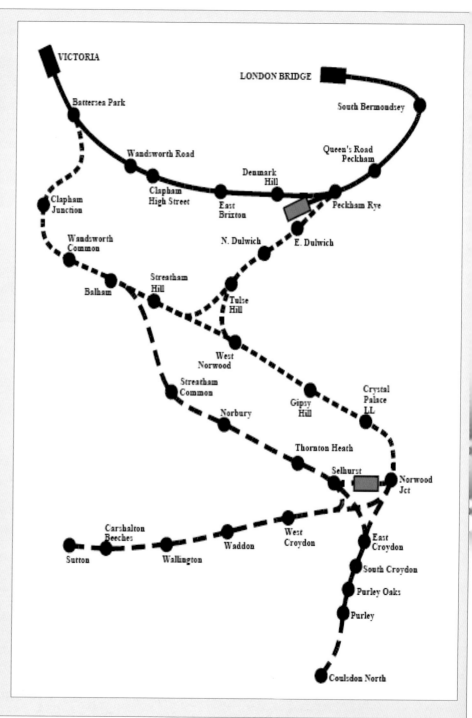

The South London Line

When Dawson submitted his report in 1904 the LBSCR Board instructed him to prepare detailed specifications and to call for tenders for the first project; electrifying part of the South London Line from Battersea Park to Peckham Rye, where a depot for the new electric multiple unit fleet, consisting of a carriage shed and an electrical repair shop, would be built in the vee of the junction with the line to Tulse Hill.

Engineering contractors Robert W. Blackwell & Co. Ltd., who specialised in tramway electrification projects, won the main contract and the order for the electrical equipment was placed with Allgemeine Electricitäts Gesellschaft (AEG) of Berlin.

Satisfied with progress over the preceding year, the LBSCR Board expanded the contract in 1906 to include the remainder of the route into the termini at London Bridge and Victoria.

On viaducts, where there was insufficient room for cantilevered structures or where the loadings on the supporting structures needed to be kept to a minimum, the electrification engineers used overhead gantries to support the catenary. In its promotional material the LBSCR branded the new service the 'Elevated Electric', an American term for their new above-street electric rapid-transit systems, the justification presumably being that most of the South London Line ran on arches at roof level. At Clapham Road, looking eastwards towards the now-closed East Brixton station on 9 July 1908, the pawnbroking, money-lending and secondhand furniture business to the right of the tracks testifies to the economic decline of the area as London's suburbs continued to expand southwards.

This page, top - *The newly completed switch cabin at Denmark Hill stands ready to receive its power supply equipment on 9 July 1908. The London Electric Supply Corporation fed power from its Deptford power station to the railway at Peckham distributing room and at the Queens Road switch cabin. A distributor cable ran the length of the South London Line, the high tension inner core feeding lineside switch cabins whilst the uninsulated outer was bonded to each running rail to form the return.*

This page, bottom - *On the same date local builder J&A Oldham of New Cross Road was in the early stages of constructing the switch cabin at South Bermondsey.*

Opposite - *Catenary masts had not made their way as far east as Peckham Rye by 9 July 1908 but work is well advanced on the switch cabin to the right of the picture and opposite the signalbox. In the distance the LCDR Catford Loop line, which had been running parallel with the South London Line on its northern side, crosses by means of a flyover and sweeps away towards Nunhead.*

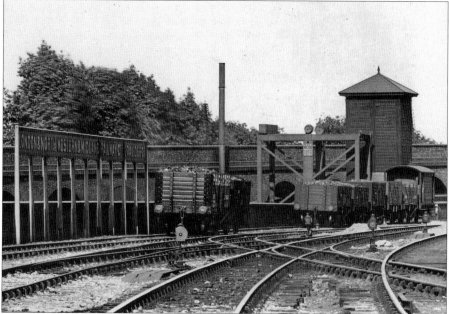

Above - *A cruel enlargement from the image opposite but included to show detail of the 'London & North Western & Midland Railway Cos. Coal Depot'. The private owner wagon visible nearest the camera would appear to be 'P H Carter / Garner', or similar.*

Above - *By 20 November 1908 work was underway on the new electric train depot and workshops located in the 'vee' of Peckham Rye Junction...........(the locomotive visible is C2 class No. 451)..............and* **(opposite top)** *cantilever catenary masts had been erected along the adjacent line towards Denmark Hill. At Peckham Rye Junction the classification of the lines change; the Down South London Line becomes the Up Atlantic Line, so named because it spans Atlantic Road as it passes over the LCDR's Chatham main line. Both views show temporary sidings laid to accommodate works traffic.*

Opposite bottom - *Denmark Hill looking towards East Brixton on 20 November 1908. Rolling insulators mounted in trunnions on the upper edge of the support structure will carry the catenary wires, a pair for each track, which passed over the supports.*

This page, left - *East Brixton looking towards Denmark Hill on the same date, 20 November 1908. In the distance, a start has been made on installing the wiring over the Up line.*

This page, bottom - *At Clapham Road (now Clapham High Street) on 20 November 1908, the galvanised steel double catenary wires and droppers are in place over each line. The grooved copper contact wire - or 'trolley wire' as it was then known in accordance with contemporary tramway terminology - is in place, but not yet tensioned, over the Down line but has not yet been installed over the Up line. The LCDR Chatham main line is on the left. As the photographic plate was being exposed, the signal dropped to 'clear' for an Up South London Line train from the East Brixton direction.*

Opposite - *Looking in the opposite direction, cables, staging and temporary sheds clutter the platform at Clapham Road. The next section is clear for the awaited Up train. The building on the left was part of the Voltaire Road premises of WR Sykes Interlocking Signal Co. Ltd. The Sykes' Lock and Block system was widely used by the LBSCR and other companies to regulate their intensive suburban traffic. It electrically locked the section signal of each signalbox so that it could not be cleared until a preceding train had passed the home signal of the next box in advance. The system worked well and doubtless prevented many accidents caused by signalmen's errors. However it could fail, locking the signals at Danger and causing major hold-ups. Consequently there was an emergency 'back lock release' facility to enable signalmen to keep traffic moving. One such accident caused by a signalman's error was to happen at Battersea Park when, on 2 April 1937, the 7:30 a.m. London Bridge to Victoria service via Tulse Hill was waiting in the platform for the 7:37 a.m. from London Bridge via Peckham to precede it over the converging junction and on into Victoria. The signalman at Battersea Park became confused about the sequence of trains on the busy main line, overlooked the waiting 7:30 a.m. from London Bridge and assumed that his Sykes instrument, which had correctly locked the signal in the rear, had failed. He used a key to release the locking and cleared his home signal for the 7:31a.m. service from Coulsdon North. This train was not booked to stop at Battersea Park and ran into the rear of the waiting train at about 35mph. Ten people were killed and 59 others were injured.*

This page - *The overhead wiring work is complete at Wandsworth Road on 20 November 1908. The catenary is designed to provide some flexibility with a minimum of hard spots. Double support wires and double insulation, with all insulators in compression rather than tension, provided a high degree of both mechanical and electrical safety. Offsetting the insulators from the centre-line of the track mitigated the effects of hot gases from steam locomotive chimneys but even so the LBSCR was to find that insulators would need replacing much more frequently on those of its electrified lines that also carried intensive steam-hauled passenger and freight traffic.* **Inset -** *Contractor advertising details.*

Opposite - *The catenary was divided into sections every mile or so, usually at stations. Each section gap was bridged by a switch cabin, providing the means to isolate a faulty section without disabling the power supply to the entire line. At Wandsworth Road the switch cabin is just visible to the left, with power cables supplying each side of the insulated sections beneath the overhead support gantry.*

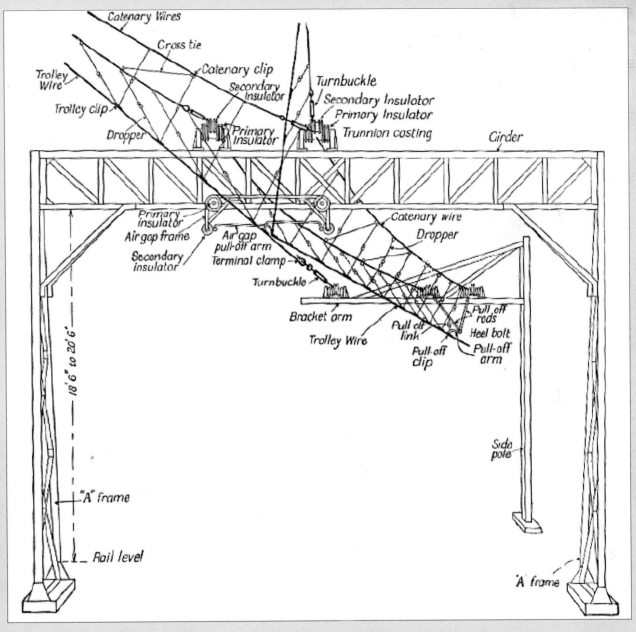

Left - *Insulators were also needed to separate 'up' and 'down' line sections at crossovers, as at East Brixton station, which was closed and demolished in 1976. Electrified crossovers were also provided at Battersea Park, Clapham Road, Denmark Hill and Peckham Rye to enable trains to reverse either side of an incident. Experience gained during a period of test running in 1909 showed that these original designs of sectional insulator caused flashing and knocking of the rolling stock bow collectors.*

Above - *To overcome this difficulty, Dawson and the LBSCR developed and patented the "air gap" insulator, whereby the catenary for the two sections ran parallel for a short distance, with the collector bow of a train briefly in contact with both.*

At some locations, such as the footbridges at Wandsworth Road station **(opposite)** *and Ferndale Road* **(above),** *there was insufficient clearance to carry the standard catenary. Here the live construction was just two inches deep and both the air clearance between it and the bridge structure and the gap between the loading gauge and the underside of the live wire were reduced to four inches. The collector bows on the trains were almost flat as they passed beneath yet there was never any problem.*

Opposite page - *The solution adopted for the bridge spanning Atlantic Road and the LCDR Brixton station was to add catenary support brackets above the existing wind tie girders. The trolley wire passed underneath the wind ties and was braced to maintain alignment and structural clearance on the sharp curve.*

Above - *At Factory Junction, just north of Wandsworth Road, the electrified Atlantic lines on the left curve away towards Battersea Park. Just beyond the signalbox the Ludgate lines also diverge to the left to pass beneath the Atlantic line viaduct and connect the LCDR lines to the LBSCR and LSWR lines at Clapham Junction and to the West London Line. Originally built to enable the LSWR to exercise running powers over the LCDR route to Ludgate Hill, these lines were by now primarily used for transfer freights and for through passenger services from midland and northern cities to Kent seaside resorts. A freight train from the GWR's South Lambeth goods depot awaits its path on to the Chatham main line. Though still separate legal entities the LCDR and its long-time rival the South Eastern Railway were by now operated as a single business under the control of the South Eastern and Chatham Railway (SECR) Joint Managing Committee.*

Soot-stained Battersea Park is given a fresh coat of paint on 20 November 1908 in readiness for the new electric service. Painters' ladders stand in the Down line four-foot and a trestle between a pair of tall stepladders is perched precariously on the platform edge a few feet away from a steam-hauled South London Line train to London Bridge standing on the Up line.

Many off-peak trains terminated at Battersea Park, doubtless irritating those passengers travelling to Victoria and encouraging their desertion to the new electric tram services. Both South London Line platforms were therefore fully signalled for eastbound departures.

The overhead wiring has not yet been installed here, though a few cables are strung casually over the supporting girders.

Opposite and top right - *Some signals, such as these at the south end of Battersea Park station, were obscured by the overhead line equipment and had to be relocated. In this undated view the Up line trolley wire has not yet been completely attached to the catenary.*

Bottom right - *The obscured signals were replaced by a new type of Sykes electrically operated, illuminated 'enclosed semaphore signal'. One was mounted under the canopy at the end of the Down platform, the other on a handy bridge abutment just beyond the end of the reversible Up platform. The overhead wiring is still only partially installed. (Two passengers in Edwardian dress gaze unsmilingly at the photographer as they await an Up train to Victoria.)*

Job done! Newly repainted Battersea Park station with the overhead line equipment in place. The stump of the old Down signal post carries a repeater for the Up starter. In the distance, at the Victoria end of the platform, Battersea Park signalbox spans the Brighton main line 'slow' tracks.

South London Line Rolling Stock

The original rolling stock for the South London Line was built in 1908-09 in the Metropolitan Amalgamated Railway Carriage and Wagon Co.'s Saltley factory and comprised eight 3-car sets, configured Driving Motor Brake Third (DMBT), Trailer First (TF), DMBT. The cars in each unit were numbered sequentially, e.g DMBT 3201, TF 3202, DMBT 3203, etc.

DMBTs were to LBSCR diagram 280 and weighed a massive 54 tons tare. The Trailer Firsts were to LBSCR Diagram 65 and weighed 31 tons tare. With 9ft wide and 60ft long bodies, these cars were larger than either the LBSCR's contemporary steam stock or its later builds of electric stock and appeared to owe more to European practice than to the LBSCR's contemporary steam stock. The main side members of the underframes were riveted plate girders, with the bottom flange cranked down between the bogies and apertures in the web to give access to underfloor equipment. The 8ft wheelbase bogies were of the Fox type, with the main members formed from steel pressings.

The new trains were fitted with the Westinghouse automatic air brake in accordance with the LBSCR's enlightened decision to standardise on this system following the 1875 Newark brake trials. Air from the main reservoirs also operated the electro-pneumatic traction control switchgear and raised and lowered the collector bow.

A panelled exterior, finished in LBSCR's 'main-line' umber and cream livery further enhanced the imposing effect of these massive vehicles. Each seating bay had a door on either side with droplights controlled by the traditional leather strap and with ventilators above. Hopper-type opening toplights above each side window provided additional supplies of fresh air.

The LBSCR went to considerable lengths to guard against the dangers of high-voltage electricity - aluminium earthing strips are fitted to the roof as a safety precaution in case the live catenary ever came into contact.

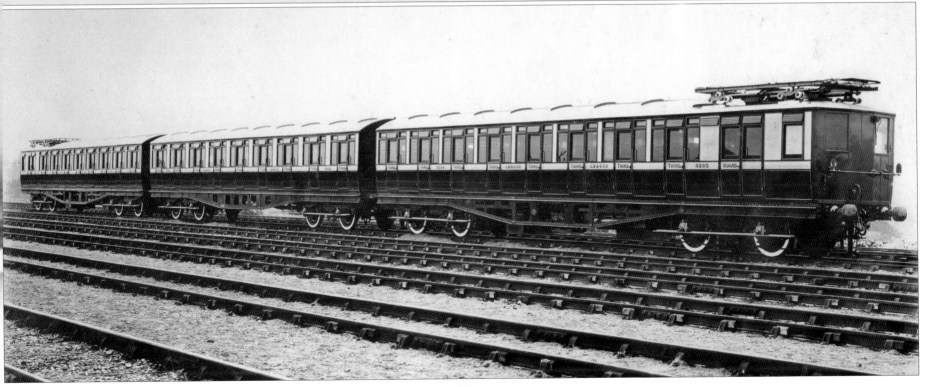

This page - *Each DMBT had a pair of collector bows - one for each direction - mounted on the flattened roof at the outer end of the car above the driving compartment and guard's van area. As there was no power bus-line connecting the two DMBTs, the unit operated with bows on each DMBT raised in the trailing position and the bows were lowered and raised automatically when the driver operated the reverser switch. From the bow, the current was fed through fuses, lightning arrestors and an automatic circuit breaker to two underframe-mounted traction transformers and an auxiliary transformer, tappings from which fed carriage lighting, control and air compressor systems. Rather surprisingly, given the ready availability of electric power, the trains originally had no heaters.*

Opposite - *All four axles of each DMBT were powered, each being driven through 4.24:1 reduction gears by an AEG motor with a one-hour rating of 115hp, located within the frame of the 8ft bogie with one end supported by bearings on the axle and the other by springs attached to the bogie's central transom. The motors were of the Winter-Eichberg 'compensated repulsion' type - a technique used on early single-phase a.c. motors to reduce flashovers between the armature coil and the commutator segments. The traction transformers supplied increasing voltages to the motors in five steps up to a maximum of 250 Volts. The switches for these steps were actuated by the master controller operating electro-pneumatic switches and the reverser on each DMBT was similarly operated electro-pneumatically. In this view of a traction motor bogie the leaf springs have not yet been fitted to the side-frames above the axle-boxes.*

The high-tension feed from the collecting bow and its associated switchgear was housed in two fireproof asbestos-lined steel cubicles that occupied the off-side position adjacent to a half-cab for the driver. The doors of these cubicles were interlocked with the collector bow to ensure that they could not be opened whilst the bow was raised and they mechanically earthed all of the high-voltage equipment when in the open position.
A diagonal partition separated the driver's half-cab from the guard's van area. This incorporated a conventional door as well as a curious semicircular panel around the handbrake pedestal and wheel. This panel could be rotated so as to place the handbrake pedestal in the driving compartment when the cab was leading or in the guard's area when at the rear of a train.

This page - *Internally all of the cars had an open plan layout to encourage passengers to board quickly and then seek a seat but they had side passageways rather than the more usual centre aisle. This was a new format for the LBSCR but was similar to the layout of the electric rolling stock on the Liverpool Overhead Railway. The South London cars had panelling beneath the transverse luggage racks to give a more enclosed, compartment-like ambience. Two carbon-filament electric ceiling lamps lit each seating bay. Each of the two 4-bay saloons to the rear of the DMBT driving and guard's compartments had a full-width seat at the outer end, providing a total of 66 (later counted as 82) passengers. The side aisle was to the right in the leading saloon, switching to the left in the rear (non-smoking) saloon and the two saloons were separated by a full-height, full-width partition with a communicating door on the right hand side.*

Overleaf - *The Trailer Firsts had 56 seats in nine semi-open bays, four smoking and five non-smoking, again with partition and door between and with the side aisle transposed at the 5th bay. Having abolished Second Class on the new South London Line trains, the company had hoped to encourage former users to 'trade up' to First-Class by offering season tickets valid for the entire line for just £7-5s-0d, compared to £5-10s-0d for Third-Class. However, demographic changes to the inner suburban area had reduced the potential First Class market and patronage was much lower than expectations. There was a dramatic growth in traffic on the line after electrification but it resulted in overcrowding in Third-Class at peak times and far too many vacant First-Class seats at all times. In view of these results the original eight 3-car units were disbanded during 1910-11 and the DMBTs were each paired with a Driving Trailer Composite (DTC) car. Thereafter, 'SL' stock trains, as they became known to distinguish them from later a.c. fleets, ran as two, four, or six cars according to demand and cars were no longer formed into semi-permanent units. The displaced Trailer Firsts were converted for steam locomotive haulage, lavatories were installed in the former central seating bay, and they were reallocated to the Brighton main line, renumbered as 167-174, later SR 7644-7651 (SR Diagram 524). Due to their wide bodies - 9ft 3ins over handrails - they were prohibited from operating through Crystal Palace tunnel. However, in a remarkably diverse career, these cars were to undergo a further conversion in 1929-30 to 2-car d.c. units for the Wimbledon-West Croydon line.*

The new electrification infrastructure and rolling stock was subjected to eleven months of trials before public services commenced on 1 December 1909. Well wrapped against a cold day, LBSCR senior staff and invited dignitaries sample the new service. The horizontal bar below the cab windows was rotated by a handle inside the cab to display either a white disc or an LV (last vehicle) indication on the left hand side in the direction of travel. Electrification came none too soon for the LBSCR. The City and South London tube line had been extended to Clapham Common in 1900 and in the same year the London County Council had obtained general powers to electrify the South London tram network. By 1908 bright new electric trams were offering a high frequency service directly from South London to the City and the West End for a fare of one (old) penny. The LBSCR's dingy steam-hauled suburban trains could not compete and South London Line passenger numbers dropped from eight million in 1903 to just three million in 1908. The new service offered a 15 minute frequency on weekdays and an end-to-end journey time of 24 minutes compared to 36 minutes for the former steam service. Traffic began to recover at once, rising by 50% within the first month. In 1910 7.5m passengers used the new 'Elevated Electric' and by 1922 annual carryings on the South London Line were 12 million.

Top left - *A South London Line train approaches the disused Grosvenor Road station on the climb from Victoria Station to the bridge over the Thames shortly after the commencement of electric passenger services. Originally a ticket-collecting platform for Up trains, Grosvenor Road station opened to the public in 1870 and closed in 1907. In service the original South London sets were numbered 1E to 8E until they were disbanded in 1910-11.*

Top right - *At Victoria, the five easternmost platforms in the LBSCR station were electrified but as these were of double length, with two 'middle roads' to enable trains from the inner platform to pass others standing at the southern end of the station, there were effectively nine platform faces available for electric trains. Standard minimum clearances for the overhead line equipment were set at ten inches; four inches between the loading gauge and the underside of the contact wire, two inches for flexing of the catenary and four inches from the catenary to the structure. A couple more inches could be won by substituting a rigid bar for flexible catenary under some low bridges. However, under Ebury Bridge and Elizabeth Bridge on the approaches to Victoria and Eccleston Bridge over the terminus platforms clearance was so limited that earthed sections had to be used, with insulated neutral sections either side. Because the live contact wires within the station were set some 19 ft 9 ins above rail level to allow men safe access to the roofs of steam trains, the insulated neutral sections either side of Eccleston Bridge were formed of 'T' section steel runners that dropped the wire 5 ft 10 ins to at a gradient of 1 in 10. With the aid of a 25mph speed restriction the rolling stock collector bows performed the necessary gymnastics without bouncing.*

Left - *The approaches to Victoria station with the overhead line equipment in place. The nearest gantry shows the 'air gap' method of dividing the catenary into sections, with the wires of two adjacent sections running parallel for a short distance to enable collector bows to make the transition smoothly.*

The Crystal Palace Lines

The LBSCR's accountants calculated that the company earned a 10% return on its capital investment in the electrification of the South London Line - a figure that needs to be taken with a small pinch of salt as the rolling stock was entirely financed from the Repairs and Renewals Fund and therefore did not appear in the capital account.

Be that as it may, the Board needed no further convincing of the financial merits of electrification and authorised further extensions, from Peckham Rye via Tulse Hill and from Battersea Park via Streatham Hill to Crystal Palace and onwards via Norwood Junction to a new electric depot.

The new electric depot at Norwood Junction takes shape. The lines from Crystal Palace to Norwood Junction were electrified to provide access to the depot and some passenger services terminated at Norwood Junction station rather than Crystal Palace. A total of ten electrified sidings were provided, of which three were extended through the depot itself, with the remainder of the building used for workshops. In addition the 'in and out roads' and the running lines between Norwood Junction and a point just short of Selhurst station were electrified, enabling trains to enter the depot from either direction - this view shows the approach from Selhurst. Pitted 'dead end' sidings for stabling and minor maintenance are under construction to the left of the building. Power for lighting and workshop machinery was supplied through transformers from the traction distribution supply cables. These a.c. servicing facilities later became part of the Southern Railway's Selhurst d.c. depot complex.

Right - *The lines from London Bridge via New Cross Gate and Sydenham and from Norwood Junction converge to the west of Crystal Palace station. The Sydenham line on the right was not electrified throughout but the catenary was extended through this part of the station to turn-back crossovers and to two berthing sidings between the widely-spaced platforms. Gipsy Hill's Up Distant signal, an electrically operated Sykes enclosed semaphore, stands at the entrance to the 746-yard tunnel.*

Below - *Cable laying in Crystal Palace Tunnel.*

Below - *Intensive activity on the approach to Crystal Palace Low Level station from the Norwood Junction direction as muscle power hoists a post for a re-sited signal into place. As well as the two running lines on the left, the bay platforms and siding on the right were also electrified to provide stabling facilities. The skyline is dominated by the imposing station building above the platforms of the original branch line from Sydenham. Behind it stands Sir Joseph Paxton's Crystal Palace.*

Opposite - *Meanwhile, work continues to install the overhead line equipment between the Norwood Junction line platforms at Crystal Palace, which lacked the magnificence of the original part of the station. Unusually the insulated trunnions supporting the catenary are below, rather than above the nearest gantry as the height of the live construction reduces to pass beneath the footbridge.*

Left - *Under bowler-hatted supervision, wiremen install lineside equipment opposite the signalbox at Crystal Palace.*

Right - *The clearance under the footbridge at West Norwood station was so tight that the live catenary consisted of just the trolley wire stretched taut between supports on either side. The enamel advertisement for Pears Soap promises the workmen a matchless complexion but, after this job, they are more likely to want a mug of Mazawattee Tea.*

Below - *Manpower! At West Norwood station labourers carry an electric supply cable into place.....*

Right- *....and stretch it tight as bowler-hatted officialdom looks on. These 0.5 sq. in. section copper cables, insulated with paper and lined with lead, were heavy.*

Both pages - *Apparently untroubled by safety considerations, linesmen install the overhead line catenary at West Norwood Junction, where the lines to Crystal Palace from Victoria and London Bridge via Tulse Hill converge. The overhead power supply arrangements were similar to those of the South London Line but in the light of experience, overhead structures were somewhat lighter and switch cabins more widely spaced.*

Above - *The Lansdowne Hill/Mount Villas road junction is partly over the railway at West Norwood Junction, creating an interesting problem for the overhead line engineers.*

Gantries and catenary are in place at Tulse Hill. The lines to the left link the route from London Bridge via Tulse Hill to the Victoria-Crystal Palace route, which can be seen in the background. Centre-right the as-yet unelectrified 'Portsmouth Lines' continue onwards towards Mitcham Junction and on the extreme right the Leigham Spur lines are ready for electric services on the London Bridge to Victoria via Tulse Hill route. Power from the London Electric Supply Corporation's Deptford power station was cabled from the South London Line's electrical control room at Peckham to the Tulse Hill distribution room, just visible on the extreme left, from where it was distributed by feeder cables to switch cabins that fed the line from Battersea Park to Crystal Palace and onwards to Norwood Junction and Selhurst depot. Several coal merchants operate from the yard beyond the junction - the shafts of their horse-drawn carts are just visible in the distance.

Above left and opposite page - *Workmen lay a power supply cable alongside the Portsmouth lines at Tulse Hill to link the distribution room with the Victoria-Crystal Palace chord.*

Above right - *The Crystal Palace electrification scheme included the lines from Battersea Park to West Norwood and Tulse Hill as well as the route from Peckham Rye. Within Streatham Hill (Leigham Court) tunnel the catenary was suspended from cross-beams inserted into the tunnel wall on each side. In those instances where the line is more or less level, tunnels are constructed with an artificial 'summit' to provide effective drainage beneath the tracks, as can be seen here.*

Above - *With the catenary already installed, work is in progress on changes to the track layout to the west of Streatham Hill station. The electrified Up Bay platform line and carriage road converges from the left. On the Down side the long siding, which fans out into a pair of sidings on the middle distance, was also electrified, providing room for several sets to be stabled between the peaks. Although the other sidings at Streatham Hill were not included in the LBSCR scheme, the Southern Railway later developed the site into a substantial depot for its d.c. electric fleet.*

Right - *High wire act! Linesmen install catenary at Balham Junction. Here the Crystal Palace lines (behind the photographer) converge with the four-track main line from Brighton and East Croydon. All four main lines were electrified between Balham Junction and Falcon Junction (Clapham).*

Left - *On a raw winter's day, track workers lay power supply cables in lineside conduits at Balham Junction. The hoarding on the building to the right includes an advertisement for the forthcoming Festival of Empire Imperial Exhibition and Pageant of London at Crystal Palace. Electric services from Victoria began on 12 May 1911, the opening day of the exhibition.*

Above - *Cable laying progresses through gaslit Balham station.*

Left - *Very few over-bridges needed to be replaced to accommodate the overhead line catenary. One exception was Bellevue Road bridge, just north of Wandsworth Common station with its low, single-line arches.*
The work is progressing in two stages, with a temporary timber bridge constructed on the extended northern half of the original piers whilst the other half comes down.

Right - *Wiring up the catenary at Clapham Junction. As ever, worker safety does not seem to be a priority. Presumably they were working within a possession, at least of the Up line, though the cleared platform starting signal suggests otherwise!*
Both the main and the local lines were electrified between Balham Junction and Clapham (Falcon) Junction but only the slow lines were electrified through the platforms at Clapham Junction and onwards to Battersea Park. The two West London Line platforms on the southern side of Clapham Junction station were also electrified, together with a short onward stretch and a crossover to the east of the station for reversals.

Left and above - *Between Clapham Junction and Pouparts Junction there was insufficient room for conventional gantries to support the overhead lines. Work has started on erecting the steelwork for one of the massive cantilevered structures that were installed on this stretch of line. From left to right, Pouparts Junction's Up Home signals are: 1, Up Brighton Fast to Up Battersea (giving access to Stewarts Lane Goods Depot and to the LCDR Chatham lines at Factory Junction); 2, Up Brighton Fast; 3, Up Brighton Slow to Up Battersea; 4, Up Brighton Slow to Up Brighton Fast; 5, Up Brighton Slow. Note the calling-on signals that enabled a freight train to enter the Up Battersea line under permissive block working when it is already occupied by another freight train.*

Right - *A partly-assembled steel structure frames the LBSCR Pouparts Junction signalbox. To the left, West London Junction signalbox spans the LSWR main lines.*

Left - *There was room for conventional support gantries as the Brighton main line diverged from the parallel LSWR main line before crossing it on a viaduct and continuing towards Victoria. The gantries spanned all four LBSCR lines but only the two slow lines were electrified. Traffic was not suspended whilst work progressed on the overhead line installation but a 15mph speed restriction was imposed. A steam-hauled Up LBSCR passenger train is just visible on the viaduct in the background having passed through the worksite.*

Above - *The main steelwork for the first two cantilever supports is in place. In the foreground, the assembly for the third structure lies on the side of the embankment waiting to be lifted on to its tower.*

Job done! An Up electric train from Crystal Palace to Victoria approaches Pouparts Junction. In the background a rake of LSWR steam-hauled stock stands on the sidings between the LSWR Main and Windsor Lines outside Clapham Yard.

Electric services from Victoria began on 12 May 1911, the opening day of the Festival of Empire at Crystal Palace. However electric services could not commence over the route from Peckham Rye to Tulse Hill until the London Electric Supply Corporation had installed additional power generating equipment. A limited electric service from London Bridge to Crystal Palace was operated from 1st March 1912 in order to save coal, which was in short supply because of a miners' strike, and the full service came into operation on 1 June 1912.

Trains operated every 15 minutes through the day between Victoria and Crystal Palace, every 20 minutes on the London Bridge-Crystal Palace route and hourly between London Bridge and Victoria via Tulse Hill, Streatham Hill and Clapham Junction. Additional trains ran at peak times, some reversing at Clapham Junction, and lower frequencies operated in the early morning and late evening and at weekends. Some trains running to and from Selhurst depot carried passengers between Crystal Palace and Norwood Junction.
As with the South London Line, the travelling public took to the new train services, with ridership increasing by 70%.

Unlike the LBSCR's South London Line stock, the Crystal Palace fleet had headcodes indicating the train's route to signalmen. The headcodes consisted of black metal plates with white numbers, mounted in the centre of the cab at window height and illuminated at night from above by an electric light. Route numbers were:

1	*Victoria-Crystal Palace*
2	*Victoria-Streatham Hill*
3	*Victoria-Norwood Junction*
4	*London Bridge-Crystal Palace*
5	*London Bridge-Streatham Hill, Clapham Junction or Victoria*
6	*London Bridge-Norwood Junction*

These were later supplemented by destination boards below the route numbers.

The original 'SL' cars were too large to pass through Crystal Palace tunnel so a new 'CP' fleet of 34 Driving Motor Brake Thirds (DMBT) and 68 Driving Trailer Composites (DTC) was built between 1911 and 1913. The Metropolitan Amalgamated Railway Carriage and Wagon Co. was again contracted to build the 34 DMBTs and 34 of the DTCs, the remaining 34 DTCs being built at the LBSCR's own works at Lancing.

The 'CP' fleet was built to the LBSCR's standard body width of 8ft and length of 54ft and closely resembled the LBSCR's locomotive-hauled coaches of the time, both externally and internally, with passenger accommodation in orthodox compartments without connecting aisles. As with the South London stock, there was no Second Class accommodation - the LBSCR went on to abolish Second Class on all of its suburban services, steam as well as electric, from 1st June 1911 and on all but its Continental services a year later. The 'CP' stock was liveried in plain umber, rather than the more elaborate umber-and-cream of the original SL cars.

The 34 DMBTs (LBSCR Diagram 282) were built in 1911-12. Like their predecessors on the South London Line they had girder underframes, Fox bogies and were powered by four geared, axle-hung and nose-suspended AEG motors but this time with an increased one-hour rating of 150hp.

Current collection, transformers and control equipment were similar to the earlier SL stock but the cubicle for the high-tension equipment was relocated to the rear of the guard's van. Although this would have made a full width cab feasible, the LBSCR persisted with the seemingly awkward half-cab layout for the DMBTs with the offside incorporated into the guard's van area. Passenger accommodation comprised 70 Third-Class seats in seven compartments and the cars weighed 51 tons.

On the other hand the DTCs did have full width driving cabs and this may have been a factor in the eventual practice of running a DMBT sandwiched between two DTCs, with two such sets making up a 6-car train. Cars did not run in semi-permanently formed units and formations were fairly flexible - for example some trains were formed of 8 cars with an additional DMBT and DTC added to two 3-car sets.

Behind the driving compartment of the DTC were three First-Class compartments with four-abreast seating (24 seats) followed by five Third-Class compartments with five-abreast seating (50 seats). Unlike the motor coaches, these trailers had similar underframes and bogies to contemporary LBSCR locomotive-hauled stock. The DTCs were to Diagram 283 and weighed 24 tons.

The DMBTs were numbered 3231-3264. DTCs built by MARCW in 1911 were numbered 4001-4030 and those built in 1912 4061-4064. Cars built by Lancing in 1911 were numbered 4031-4056 and the 1913 batch took the numbers 4069-4076.

The Coulsdon & Wallington Scheme

The LBSCR Board had intended the Crystal Palace project to be a stage in a rolling programme of suburban electrification and, as part of the Crystal Palace works, the company installed overhead catenary from Norwood Junction to West Croydon and from Balham to Streatham Common.

In 1913 the LBSCR Board authorised electrification of its remaining principal suburban routes as far as Cheam and, as it was then known, Coulsdon & Smitham Downs. By the time war broke out in August 1914 new catenary had been installed from Streatham Common to the Selhurst complex and from Tulse Hill to Streatham South Junction, en route for Sutton and Cheam via Mitcham Junction. However, with Britain at war with Germany it was obviously no longer possible to obtain the equipment on order from AEG in Berlin, British manufacturing capacity was fully committed to supporting military needs and manpower was in short supply so electrification work was suspended until 1921.

The main line railways came under Government control for the duration of the war and a Railway Executive Committee, chaired by Herbert Walker, General Manager of the LSWR, co-ordinated the use of the rail industry's resources for the war effort. Army, Navy and Government personnel and goods were carried free, locomotives, rolling stock and track were shipped abroad and railway workshops were diverted from manufacturing and overhauling rolling stock and other assets on order to produce war materials. In return the Government had guaranteed the railway companies their 1913 net revenue during the war but, by 1918, the railways were faced with a massive backlog of repairs and renewals, compounded by shortages of materials and skilled labour.

Wages had soared to three times their 1913 levels and other costs had increased sharply. Although the Government had allowed fares to be increased by 50% in 1917, partly to discourage unnecessary wartime travel, there was no political will to allow freight rates to increase now that the UK economy was sliding into a post-war recession. Far from being able to resume investment projects such as electrification, the railway companies faced an alarming gap between operating costs and revenues. It was not until the Government provided capital investment guarantees in 1921 that the LBSCR Board was able to authorise resumption of the work on electrifying the lines to Coulsdon and to Sutton via Wallington.

In that same year the Government legislated to amalgamate the main line railway companies into four Groups - of these, the new Southern Railway's principal constituents were to be the London & South Western Railway, the London, Brighton and South Coast Railway, the South Eastern Railway and the London, Chatham and Dover Railway - the last two still legally separate companies despite the fact that the South Eastern and Chatham Joint Committee that had run them as a single entity for over 20 years.

Although the LBSCR's Coulsdon & Wallington scheme was still incomplete when the new Southern Railway came into existence on 1st January 1923, work was so far advanced that the new Board allowed it to go ahead whilst it decided on a future standard electrification system.

The London Electric Supply Corporation again provided power for the newly electrified routes, cabled from the supply point at New Cross Gate to Gloucester Road Junction, near Selhurst, from where it was distributed to switch cabins along the three arms of the route in a similar manner to the LBSCR's previous electrifications.

Catenary is in place through East Croydon station The new electric services to Sutton and to Coulsdon North (as Coulsdon and Smitham Downs had become) started operating on April 1st 1925 - a rather chaotic day as fate conspired to bring down a conductor wire near Battersea Park that morning. The timetable provided a 20 minute regular-interval service frequency over each route, with longer train formations at peak times and with a half-hourly frequency at lunchtimes, late evenings and on Sundays.

Perhaps with eventual electrification of its main lines in mind, the LBSCR adopted a different format for its Coulsdon & Wallington rolling stock. The trailers and driving trailers were generally similar to those already in service on the South London and Crystal Palace routes but they were powered by short-framed motor luggage vans (MLV) instead of motored passenger cars.

With the disruption caused by the Great War, the CW fleet has a complex history. Of 42 Driving Trailer Composites built between 1914 and 1921 only two went straight into service as electric cars, added to the Crystal Palace fleet. The other 40 entered service between 1919 and 1921 as locomotive-hauled cars, 20 of which were later taken into the CW fleet.

40 Driving Trailer Thirds were built in 1923 on 48ft underframes with a driving compartment and eight Third Class compartments seating 80 and weighing 25 tons. Of these, 20 were supplied by the former LBSCR carriage works at Lancing and were delivered in LBSCR umber, 17 had bodies built at Eastleigh on Lancing underframes and were painted in Southern olive green and three were built by a contractor, the Metropolitan Carriage, Wagon and Finance Co. (MCWF), and were also green.

20 Trailer Composites were built in 1923 on 48ft underframes with four First Class compartments (32 seats) and four Third Class compartments (40 seats) and weighing 24 tons. Ten were built by Lancing and out-shopped in LBSCR umber, seven by Eastleigh and three by MCWF, all delivered in Southern green.

In 1923-24 MCWF built 21 motor luggage vans. Nicknamed 'milk vans', they were 38ft 5ins long, 8ft wide, weighed 62 tons tare and were numbered 10101-10121. They had two massive bogies with an 8ft 9in wheelbase, each powered by two GEC (Oerlikon) force-ventilated compensated series motors, each with a one-hour rating of 250hp.

Behind full-width driving cabs at each end were equipment rooms, each housing a main transformer and associated control systems, with ventilating fans to force-cool the transformers and motors. Two pairs of collector bows, one for each transformer for each direction of travel, were mounted on the roof - as with the earlier motor coaches these were raised and lowered by compressed air. A guard's compartment and luggage area occupied the centre of the vehicle between the equipment bays.

Though they had fully-equipped driving compartments the MLVs usually ran sandwiched between pairs of trailers; Driving Trailer Third, Driving Trailer Composite, Motor Luggage Van, Trailer Composite, Driving Trailer Third, giving a total of 64 First- and 240 Third-Class seats.

The headcode number series for the Crystal Palace services was extended to include the new routes:

7	Victoria-Selhurst via Streatham Common
8	Victoria-West Croydon via Crystal Palace
9	Victoria-Sutton via Streatham Common
10	Victoria-East Croydon via Crystal Palace
11	Victoria-Coulsdon North via Streatham Common
12	Victoria-Coulsdon North via Crystal Palace

In addition, an 'SL' headcode was adopted for South London Line services.

Two rakes of Coulsdon and Wallington (CW) stock stand in the stabling sidings at Coulsdon. Although the date is 28 May 1927 the leading car, Driving Trailer Third is still in LBSCR livery and bears its LBSCR running number, 3284 whereas the second car, a Driving Trailer Composite, is in Southern green.

Bibliography

'LBSCR Appendix to the Service Time Table and to the Book of General Rules and Regulations LBSCR', official publication 1922

'The London Brighton and South Coast Railway Co. 1846-1922', LBSCR official publication 1923

Bell, Richard: unpublished monographs

Brown, David: 'Southern Electric' (Volume 1) Capital Transport Press 2010

Dawson, Sir Philip: 'Electric Traction on Railways' and 'Railway Mechanical Engineering' (Vol. II), Gresham 1923

Dendy Marshall, C.F. revised by Kidner R.W. 'A History of the Southern Railway' (combined volume), Ian Allan 1968

Dunbar, Chas S: 'Buses, Trolleys & Trams' (2nd ed), Hamlyn 1968

Golding, Brian, 'A Pictorial Record of Southern Electric Units Drawings and Plans', Noodle Books 2009

Hamilton Ellis, C: 'The London, Brighton and South Coast Railway', Ian Allan 1960

Harvie, Kenneth G. 'Tramways of South London and Croydon 1899-1949', 5th edition London Borough of Lewisham 1975

Mitchell, Vic and Smith, Keith , 'South London Line - London Bridge to Victoria', Middleton Press 1975

Moody, G.T. 'Southern Electric' (4th ed), Ian Allan 1968

A three-car formation of CP stock at Victoria, awaiting departure to Crystal Palace.

The end of 'The Overhead'

Top - *Recorded in the last week of operation, a Coulsdon North, via Thornton Heath, service recorded at Victoria.*

Bottom - *The final day, Sunday 22 September 1929. Driver Bill Mann has charge of a five-coach train of 'CW' (motor-van stock), forming the 12.10 am Victoria to Coulsdon North via Streatham Common.*

The 'CP' and 'CW' passenger coaches, together with the 'SL' driving trailers will be rebuilt as 3-car d.c. suburban electric units whilst the original wide-bodied 'SL' stock will see out its remaining life as 2-car d.c. electric units for the South London and Wimbledon-West Croydon lines. The 'CW' motor luggage vans will eventually be rebuilt as massive bogie brake vans - their steady riding characteristics and sure-footed braking capability endearing them to goods train guards.